into *soul* scapes *of being*

SARAH SAMEERA

*dedicated to
every being that still dares
to live this life from the wild place of soul
& to my inner child,
who dreamed of writing her own books,
for as long as I can remember*

into soulscapes of being

cycles

creation's child

soul calling

way of love

sacred descent

rising into destiny

inner revolution

belonging

prologue

This book was birthed from the shatters of broken dreams. At least I thought so when I first started to put it all together. Most of these words were written in the years 2019 - 2022 while living on the island of Koh Phangan, Thailand. A bunch of notes scribbled into some of my dozens of journals. Not with the intention to ever be published, but simply because I do not know any other way to exist on this planet.

Creating for me comes very close to breathing – if I do not write or sing or dance or allow creativity to pour through me in any other shape or form – I cease to feel alive. It is my way to make sense of this strange experience of being human; it is my prayer, my therapy, my greatest love and my purpose all at once.

And while around us the entire world was descending into chaos and fear, I found myself stranded on a small crystal island in the Andaman Sea – a place of such incredible beauty that it can almost feel like tasting paradise at times. Many times I wondered how on earth I ended up here – but most of all I was grateful beyond words to be in a place like this in a moment like that. In some ways, it felt like a childhood dream came true – living in a wooden house in the forest with a dog and a cat on a tropical island.

And because the human world was held on pause for some time, all that was left to do was dance and sing and read and write and cuddle and eat fruits and swim and play and explore. As if life was finally giving me the permission to let my heartbeat sync to the slow, steady pace of Mother Earth beneath my bare feet and immerse my entire being in the lifegiving nectars of creation – simply for the sake of creating.

Nature was speaking clearly to me in these times. She was calling out to my wild heart – into action, into creation, into service. I did not know in what way, but I was open to surrendering. And when I asked, all she replied was:

Open your voice. Share your truth. Sing your song. And something did open from someplace deep within me, like the gates of a river that were lifted by some unseen hand.

Songs started to flood through me, without me ever asking for them. Without me ever intending to even write any song. It was a gift coming from someplace beyond me and I knew it wasn't mine to keep. And when I sang those songs to the people around me, I was moved by something bigger than me – making me feel more alive, more in love, more on purpose than ever in my entire life. And everyone around me was touched by that same force. I found my medicine – or rather my medicine found me. And even though it scared me, I was committed to sharing it with the world.

But then 2021 hit me like my own personal apocalypse. I was just performing at my first festival, about to start my own band. Dreams seemed to blossom that I did not even dare to dream of. But then – just like for many of us within those years – the darkness arrived and ripped my life into pieces. And I thought I had made friends with her before – the dark night that lived beneath my skin. Yet what I've met before were just the shadows of my own shadow self.

This time life invited me into an initiation into my own underworld that was beyond anything I had ever experienced before. There I was, paralyzed in pain and in fear – watching the entire story of my life flipped upside down. Suddenly paradise had turned into hell. Everything that I was ever scared of hit me all at once. Everything I've ever been running away from finally got hold of me. Everything that was dear to me seemed to be falling apart right in front of my eyes – who I thought I was, who I called my soul family, what felt like home to me & what I thought my biggest dreams were.

But the most heartbreaking thing of it all was that in the arrival of this dark night – my voice completely disappeared. It felt like I've lost the one thing in my life that fulfilled me the most, the one thing that healed me in ways like nothing else. Just when I needed it the most. I was overwhelmed by grief and shame, as I felt like I failed my purpose and had to watch opportunities of my dreams crumble into pieces right in front of my eyes.

That's when I started writing this book. Because I knew I had to create something if I wanted to get better. Because I knew there was nothing more healing on this entire planet for me than to bathe myself in that eternal river of creation – to let my wounds be washed free until my soul could breathe again.

And so, I started copying all the poems that I've written over the past couple of years and put them together into different books. The first one you are holding in your hands right now – the beginning of a life's work of retrieving the truth of my being and offering that to this world.

These poems were the reminders of my soul, that I needed to hear myself in one of the darkest, most challenging moments of my life. They were the rescue rope woven from the truth that my mind had forgotten, saving me from drowning within my own internal nightmare. They were the notes from my soul to my little human self, reminding me of who I truly was, just when I felt as if I lost exactly that. They were the beginning of the resurrection of my own once silenced voice.

This book is part of the reason, why I made it through that dark night; a current of that river of grace that carried me to the other shore – more at peace, more at home and more empowered within myself than ever before. And with a voice that has returned – with a fullness and depth that she had not carried before.

It is the living proof that each journey into the darkness holds unknown gifts to be uncovered by our bare souls. We may not see them at that moment – but once we rise again, we do not come empty-handed. Because right there in our internal underworld we find the hidden treasures of our soul. This book is one of them. If my voice had not disappeared, these words would probably not even exist the way they do. And if I had not crumbled into dust and into dirt, I would not have needed their medicine the way I did.

So, this is my prayer for this book.

That these words may heal you just as they healed me.
That they may give you the courage to follow your own
calling of soul, no matter how bone-shaking scary that can feel
at times.
That they may be a spark of remembrance in those moments
when you feel like drowning in the amnesia of who you truly
are.
That they may carry you through the dark night and help you
to remember the sacredness of every single chapter of this
journey, of both the ones of struggle and the ones of joy.
That they may feed you with the devotion to truly believe in
your own dream and live that sacred vision with every step
upon this earth.
That they may open your eyes and open your heart to the
miraculous beauty of all of life and most of all – of yourself.
That they may inspire you to rewrite your own story, just as I
rewrote my story, by birthing this book into life.

So that we may all together write a brand new story for this
aching world. Because we need it. And she calls us to.

With love & gratitude,

Sarah Sameera

creation's child

and then there are those moments when you remember. when you catch a piece of sun with your bare feet kissing the soft morning dew. when you lose your mind in winding forest paths until you feel the earth breathing through the trees dancing all around you. when you listen to a song that makes your heartbeat sync as one with that all-encompassing rhythm of creation. when you return into the arms of the beloved until your ribcage cracks wide open and those waterfalls of longing carry you back where you belong. when you look up to the stars and suddenly you see yourself and how tiny and insignificant and infinite and miraculous you are all at once. when you see out into this world through the eyes of a newborn child and the terrifying beauty of simply being here and now leaves you empty of words yet filled with sheer awe. when all that's left to do is to bow down onto these bleeding knees kissing that soft soil of creation. then – you remember. that we are all just children of creation / a drop in that ever-cycling flow of the infinite / a tiny cell in this one living body called the earth / a breath that's being breathed by someone far beyond you but who somehow still lives right here underneath your skin. because somewhere deep within, don't we all still carry that exact same seed of creation that once created us?

of longing of soul

yet this soul
will always
  l o n g for the wild

for the taste
of freedom
d r i p p i n g
from a heart
b e a t i n g
of pure passion

for the sense
of sheer aliveness
p u l s a t i n g
from deep within
each core
of each piece
of this house
of sensing flesh

for that breathtaking
moment of
skin m e l t i n g
in totality
when all of life
is breathing
you

for that song
of all creation
t o u c h i n g you
right in that
space
no hand
could ever
reach

resurrected
in that moment

when you remember
how to listen

listen deeply

not with the ears but
with the courage of
a heart
b r e a k i n g
o p e n
w i d e

and there –
can't you see?

that which
you've always
longed for
is found
nowhere
but
right
here

*in that tale
of a life lived
by one who
returned
into the land of
the soul*

your own prophecy

there is
an ancient prophecy
longing
to be lived
through your
journey
on these lands

all it takes
is to
remember

that higher vision
written on
those hidden wings
of your heart

to listen
to that one
becoming song
of soul

and allow it
to dance wildly
through your flesh
and through your life

to echo
through the footprints
that you paint
upon this earth

the key
is to surrender

to your own
unique purpose
in that
one purpose
of it all

you are one
with the great web
of creation

and
your heartbeat
is the rhythm
of the
great
prophecy

creation's gift

within your body
lies the power
to grow
life

within your mind
the power
to create
anything
that you can
imagine

so why are you so scared
to simply
be
and
love
yourself?

you are a reflection
of the whole universe

*you are creation
expressing itself
in your
own
precious
uniqueness*

garden of eden

there is a whole universe within you

you are
nothing more
// nothing less
than a reflection
of everything that is

just as this world you witness
beyond those windows of your soul
is just a mere reflection
of your own internal world

so whatever
you wish to see within this world
plant within yourself first

water those seeds of love
within your self -
seeds of compassion
seeds of peace
seeds of joy

hold them in your fertile darkness
like mother earth holds all her children

nurture them
with your tears
your sweat
your breath
again // and again // and again

and then watch them grow
roots getting stronger
rising tall within your being

make space for that new life
let go of all those limitations
you once put around yourself

see those walls
that you have built -
bricks of pain and fear and
shame
stacked carefully
around your oh
so tender heart

and see -
see them for what they are

see that they are not
what you truly are

tear them down
give them to the fire
let the sun back in

*there is a whole universe
within you*

waiting for you
to be explored
and transformed
into that garden of eden
that's been sleeping
inside of you
all your life

and then -
let it grow
out into this world

let the fruits of your being
spread those seeds of love
within everything you touch

let your true essence blossom
out of the core of your very own soul

let it rise beyond anything
you've ever thought you were

because transforming our inner world
means transforming our outer world

the only true change
needs to come from within

the revolution it happens in secret
within those multiverses underneath our skin

let us remember our true nature –

that each of us
is nothing less
than a space
of infinite possibilities

and from there
let us give birth
to a new way of being

so that we
may give birth
to a new way of earth

do you dare to reclaim the birthright of your life?

dare to live

dare to listen
even to those
gentle whispers
of your naked
beating
heart

dare to trust
even in the face
of the grace
of sheer
unknown

dare to love
even when life
breaks you
down
onto
your
very
knees

dare to live
that dream
no matter how
impossible
it seems

dare to be
that miracle
in motion
that you have
come
to
be

painted by life

in a way
emotions
are just like
colours

different
tastes
/ and shades
/ and fragrances
of that experience
of life

*because
what beauty
holds a rainbow
that is
painted
only
white?*

if you look
at them
this way

why bother
clinging
or resisting?

each moment
a brushstroke
of creation

on the canvas
of your
being

perfectly
placed
in that
masterpiece
of life

the chances to be

you could have been
some speck of dust
on some distant planet
spiraling around
some odd colored sun
that we don't even
have the name for
to describe

you could have been
some tiny insect
crawling somewhere
deep beneath your feet
some place
between the dirt and mud
blessed only
- someday
sometime -
to witness
what the light means

you could have been
some blade of grass
in between
a trillion of other
blades of grass
same shape, same form, same color
one whole lifetime
growing in that
one same place
and only some moment
when the wind blows through
that blazing meadow
- just the right way -
will know what is
the ocean

but no -
by some chance
for some reason
you came to be
birthed as a human
upon this speck
of stardust called
the earth

with a body
that can move
and sense
and birth

with a mind
you can transform
and through that
even transform
the world that
you perceive

with a voice
that can speak
creation into being
that can sing
the song of life and death
in a way so unique
that there's not
a single one like yours
in the whole of
existence

with a soul
that can love
and awaken
and remember
and expand

a soul that is one
with the same essence
of everything
that is

the same essence
that could have been
anything
  A N Y T H I N G
in the infinitude
of the cosmos

but chose
to be born
as exactly
  Y O U

this unique speck
of dust
of creation

living dying paradox

your body
contains both
cosmic dust
and earthly mud

your mind
contains both
desert storms
and mountain lakes

you are
a living
dying
paradox

both a
madly creative
force of destruction
and the indestructible
force of creation
itself

an insignificant
miracle
of miraculous
significance

and some place
deep within
your soul
you'll find
the keys
to both
paradise
and
hell

poetry embodied

and when we dance
let's give ourselves
wholeheartedly
to that rhythm
which moves
all of life

and when we sing
let us be
fully empty
just as that
hollow bone
from which
creations song
is born

and when we meet
let's meet in love
like those
hopeless romantics
that still believe
in that dream
of living poetry
embodied
in skin
and in flesh

to meet
all of life
from
stripped
naked
soul
full
ness

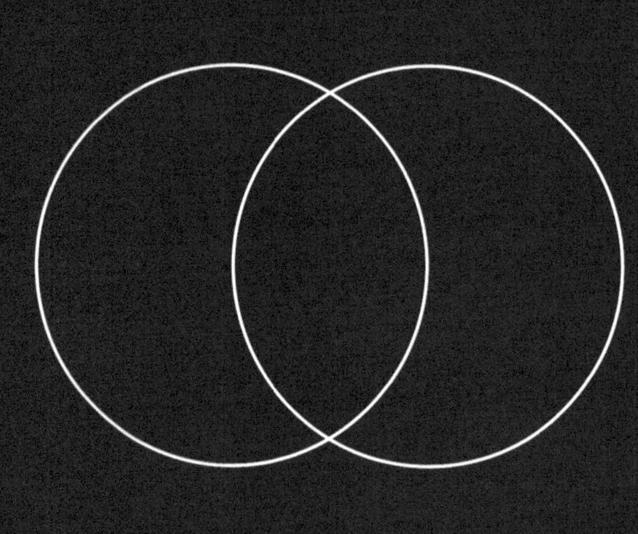

soul calling

there you stand. at the threshold to the path of your soul. where it may lead you? you may not ever know. unless you dare to walk it – that unknown road back to that queendom of inner gold. you've heard the call. you've heard it all your life. that one mysterious longing somewhere deep within your bones. a divine eternal ache that's been there way before your eyes even opened to the light of the sun. a hunger of soul – yearning … yearning … yearning … for what? … something you do not even know. call it love, call it light, call it home, call it god. whatever it may be – it is way, way bigger than everything you've ever known. yet here it is - still slumbering at the core of your very own being. and in those moments when you pause from all those struggles of being human and that divine drama we call life – it comes crawling from somewhere deep underneath your skin. whispering to you in a language only your heart can understand. but one thing you sense with every cell that shapes your being - that there is more. more to this life than what your humble eyes can see. more to this journey than your little mind could even grasp. but be prepared, my friend. this journey is not for the faint hearted. it is not a straight line. not a well paved highway. not a fast track into the life of shimmering dreams. it's much rather a bumpy, winding dirt road across rivers and mountaintops, through enchanted forest and lonely deserts, passing ancient ruins and lush green valleys filled with moss and rocks and lakes. because your soul does not care about the comfort of the known. she does not care about the preferences of your little human mind. she does not care about safety nets and logic and plan b's. for all she cares about is the evolution of your being. all she cares about is for you to return as the wholeness that you are.

ancient voices

hear them calling
from the depths
of the dreamtime

those ancient voices
hidden under
traffic noise
and the silence
of amnesia

hear them calling
from the core
of your bones

whispering the name
you carried
long before
you were born

hear them calling;
calling you
to return

written in these bones

this body is
living breathing mythology

ancient scriptures
carved into
the membrane
of the soul

each and every cell
of this house
of flesh and bones

contains
somewhere hidden
right at its
very core

the story
of the entire
cosmos

encoded
within
this very DNA

and we -
g e t
  t o
   c h o o s e

which story
do we choose
to live?

the story of fear
  or
the prophecy of soul?

*this body
is the gateway
of the
great
prophecy*

to be alive

and isn't it
so simple
in the end?

isn't that
what it is
all about?

about going
where you feel
most alive

wherever
that
may be

whatever
person
place
or passion

that keeps calling out
to your being

that calling
that sets
your soul
on fire

that calling
that makes
your heart
sing loud

that scares
your little self
deep down
unto your bones

because it's way
  W A Y bigger
than you
will ever be

so why keep on
fighting
against that
very force
that keeps
the cosmos
moving

and even
if it burns
you -

how will we ever
learn to walk
the fire

if we never
dare
to start?

it's time to jump
it's time to trust
it's time to fly

isn't it
so simple
in the end?

we came here
to be alive

so why not
live fully
boldly
unapologetically?

to simply
live
that life
that makes
your
heart
beat
full
of
life

the brave ones

if you are
running away
from what
you're scared of

you are still
in fear

whether it's
the fear
of fear
or the fear
of - whatever
it may
be

you are still
in fear

and you know what?
that's okay -
that simply means
you're
human

so why not accept
that fear
is there

[part of this wild
spiral journey
of life]

and yet
we still
can chose
to move
the way
our hearts
call us
to move

even though
there is fear

only that
it does not have
to control us
any longer

only that
it does not have
to stop us
any longer

and even
if our legs
are shaking
they still
remember
how to walk

the brave ones
are not
the ones
born fearless

the brave ones
are
the ones
that through the fear
learned
how to
thrive

keep on walking

hear your Self
whisper to yourself
gentle reminders
of what you've known
all along

you are exactly
where you need to be
with all those challenges
and blessings
with all those doubts
and hopes
and questions

because the truth is
we can never be lost

we can only feel lost
- to once again
remember

we've been
on the right track
all along

and even though
sometimes
we forget
how to simply
keep on walking

or how to follow
those gentle nudges
of our own
pulsating hearts

all ways
are always
leading us
home

and even if
sometimes
we fall off
of our path
and fight our way
through thicket
and thorns;
or walk
in circles
after circles

maybe only to remember
how good it feels

to find
our
way
back
to
a
l
i
g
n
m
e
n
t

but all of that
is part of the journey

even those
bone shattering
moments of fear
when it feels
like our own feet
are not ours
to control
any longer

even those
heartbreaking
moments of defeat
and despair
where all of our dreams
seem crumbling
c r u m b l i n g
away

but what if
dreams
can never be broken
and when it seems so
it's just their way
to change
and become?

and what if
our way
can never be lost
because it is always
right here
where we belong?

so, go on
whisper
to yourself
gentle reminders
of what you've known
all along

to keep on doing
what you're doing

to keep on walking
walking to the sun

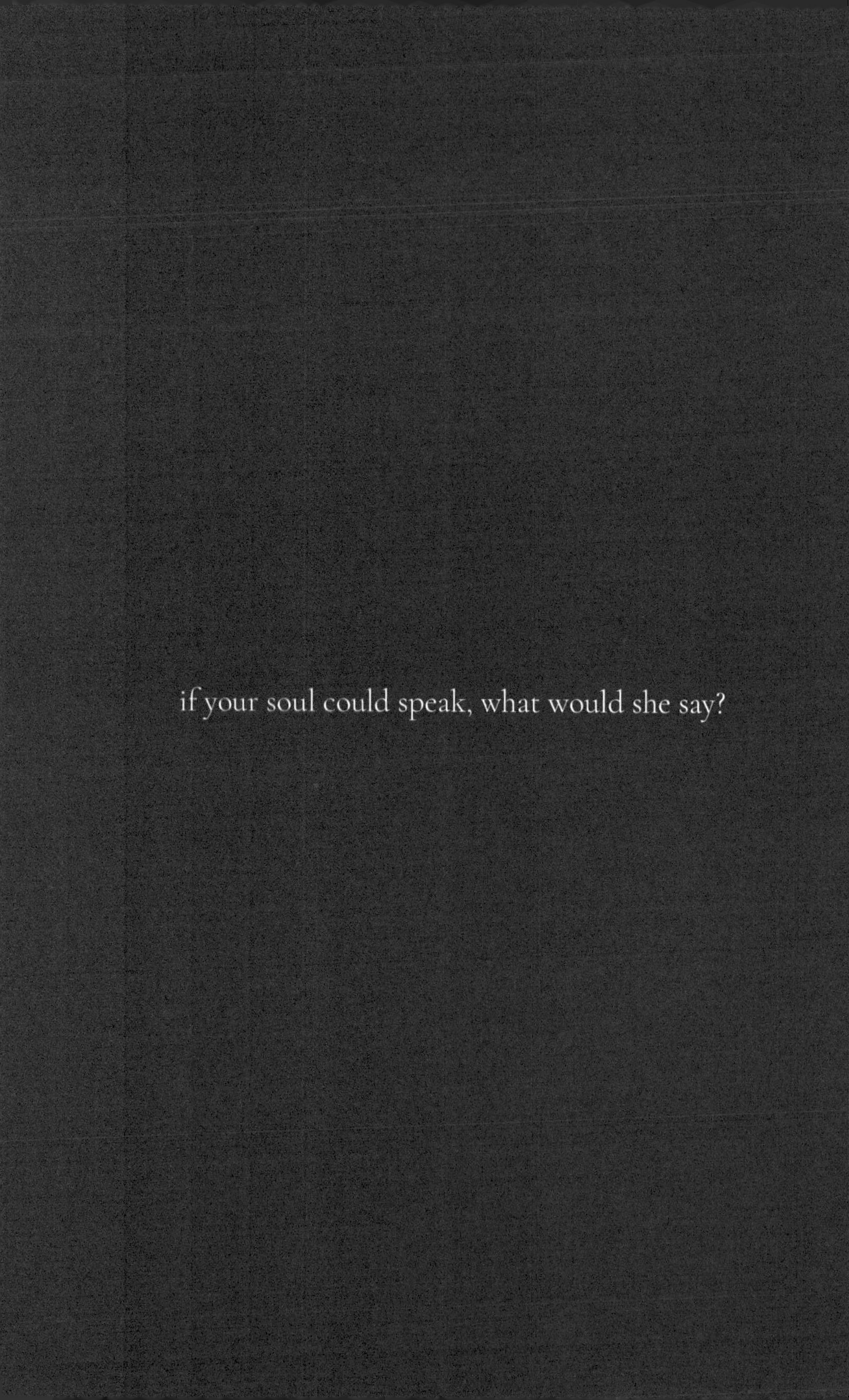
if your soul could speak, what would she say?

the maze

the maze
is not only
about finding
the center
or finding
the way
through

the maze
is about
the maze
itself

about walking
the way
through its twists
and its turns

it's about
the journey
of getting lost
and finding the way
once
again

about
each
and
every
step
of
the
path

about
the hidden secret
whispering
from the core
of it all

the way is not found
by the mind

the way
is only known
in the heart

the key to joy

the secret
to living
this life
joyfully

lies not in
always seeking happiness
or in the chase
of constant positivity

you'll find it
hidden
in the messy
and chaotic;
in the dirt
and in the mud

you'll find it
in the ability
to enjoy
the full spectrum
of this strange experience
of being human

you'll find it
in the leaning in
to the fullness
of what it means
to be alive

you'll find it
in the celebration
of both the challenges
and blessings
of both dark swamps
and holy mountains

you'll find it
in the second
you learn
to enjoy
e v e r y
s i n g l e
t e x t u r e
of this weaving
called your life

no matter
how that looks like
no matter
how that feels like

and once
you've learned
to enjoy
even
the dance
with your own
demons

just imagine
how joyful
you will feel

dancing
your way
back to the light

how to carry a vision

there is a way
I promise you
  t h e r e   i s   a   w a y

you might not see it
[yet]

because no human feet
have walked it
before you

you might not know where
it will lead you
[yet]

because not even
your wildest imagination
could most possibly
comprehend
the vast beauty of
your destiny

you might not know how to
arrive there
[yet]

but if
you have
a vision
for this earth
then there ain't no other way
than to offer it
your life

and yes,
there will be moments
where you doubt
where you scream / and stumble /
and fall

maybe just to learn
how to rise
after all

and I promise you ~
there will be
wildflowers
blooming
from your footprints
on this soil

and they will
whisper to
your soul

each step here
is leading you
home

nectar of infinity

but if
you've tasted
only once
from that
sweet nectar
of infinity

then
there is
no going back

you won't ever
forget
again

once you've tasted
only once
how it feels
to let your
consciousness
  e x p a n d ;
allowed that sense
of separation
to be d i s s o l v e d
within
the
  w h o l e

you will
forever
be hungry
for more

and even
if you try
to forget

your soul
will keep knocking
on the door
of your heart

until
that pressure
gets so big
you can
no longer hold
your true being
back

even if that
takes the prize
of all you've thought
you were

and there ~
you
get
out
of
the
way

and the river
dissolves
in the sea

ocean of being

the ocean itself
is not scared
of the waves and
the storm and
the changing
of its form

'cause in
whatever way
life is moving
its waters

the ocean remains

~

once we remember
our boundlessness
our primordial
eternity

it's finally safe

  t o
  l e t
  g o

let go
of all grasping
all resisting
to those
currents
of life
that ebb
and flow
through us

and in that moment
we surrender
into the ocean
of being

being
the infinite
itself

when grace comes around

there are
- no road signs -
at the doorway
of grace

she comes around
the corner
and sweeps you
off your feet

sometimes
cloaked as
dusty summer storms
that eat this
barren land

sometimes
hidden in
that long awaited
choir
of
these
wandering / falling
ocean
fragments

you might
curse her

//

you might
thank her

both with tears in
your eyes
beckoning
to the earth
that *s h e*
has done
her work

there are
- no road signs -
at the doorway
of grace

but you shall know
when you
have been there

dirty knees &
dirty forehead;
as you
have learned
to kiss the
ground

[and a heart both
broken & whole]

way of love

the whole world speaks about it, yet not even a million songs or words or movies could ever define its true nature. we all want it, yet we all run away from it. we all crave for it, yet when it arrives, we are terrified. hungry ghosts hunting for love in all the wrong places. because love is more than just the sweet and spicy happily-ever-after. it is more than just the moment when husband and wife meet to unite their paths of life. it is more than just the tingles on your heart's skin, before you kiss for the first time. it is even more than the unconditional bond between a mother and her child. for love is what birthed us and what will kill us once again. it is all around us, yet can only be found once we open up within. it's the answer to every question and the question that will never have an answer. it's every end and every beginning and that one sacred threat that weaves the two into one. it's both the longing and the belonging. it's both the breaking and the mending. it is that underlying current of creation that connects every single particle with all that is alive. it is the bridge into remembrance, the whispers of your heart's true yearning and the first and last rays of the sun. it is the rain that only rises to merge with the ocean once again. for love is where all comes from and where we all return to – without ever having left after all.

the way of love

*the way of love
is a dangerous path*

and there will be
the point

[again and again]

where love whispers…

are you willing
to risk
all
that you are?

are you willing
to let go
of you
of me
of that place
of the known?

are you willing
to let me in again?

for me to touch
even the places
you've tried to hide
all of your life?

are you willing
to open up
once again

to fully open
to that one
way of love?

*the way of love
is a dangerous path*

it will break down
the ego
break open
the soul

are you willing
to let love
move you
change you
transform you?

in ways you thought
were far beyond
possible

*but love can
and love will*

and it will
challenge you
and
tear you
apart

and then
when everything
seems lost

out there in the darkness
heart broken open wide

love will whisper
once again…

do you trust in me?
do you believe in me?
do you surrender
to my way?

and then
what choice is even left?

because you know
to turn around
is no more way

because
when everything fell apart
there was
only
love
left

no you
no me
no choice
to make

and there
you give up

because you are tired
of running
and tired
of fighting
against that strongest force
of all life

okay…
love hears you whisper
I am yours.

and love smiles…
you've been that all along,
my child
how could you
be here
otherwise?

walking
the
dangerous
path
of
love

just as it is

resist nothing;
not even
resistance

let everything
arise -
just as it is

this is the key
to the garden
of eden

to dive fully in
not head
but heart
first

when love returns

let love back in;
open those dusty
windows of your soul

let those wild
winds of grace
breathe life into
those shady corners
of your home

let the fragrance
of roses cracking open
~ some place deep
within your being ~
tickle your heart
to reawaken

shake those snowflakes
off your skin
and off your bones

winter is over
and
all of life
is waiting
for you

let yourself
be healed
be touched
be moved

by that
 o n e
force of love
that walked with you
all of your life

dare to become
so utterly empty
that the floods
of her grace
break into
your oh-so-thirsty heart

and let yourself
be entirely
filled
by that
very same
essence
of what
you truly are

always held

and so -
in that remembrance
that we are
 a l w a y s   held

held by that
eternal presence
of the now

all resistance
drops
away

nothing left
we need
to hold on to
any longer

as
we are
the ones
that are held

and whatever
there is
arising
within that
vast field
of consciousness

we are always safe
we are always held

held by that
deep love
of
the
now

ever worthy

a reminder
that -

your worth
is not dependent
on how other people
treat you

and the actions
of others
say so much more
about their own
sense
of worthiness
than about
yours

to dare
to fully own
your own
ever present
worth

and yet
every time
another being
reflects
your own wounds
of seeming
heart aching
unworthiness

take it
as a reminder
an invitation

to love your self
d e e p e r
f u l l e r
b o l d e r

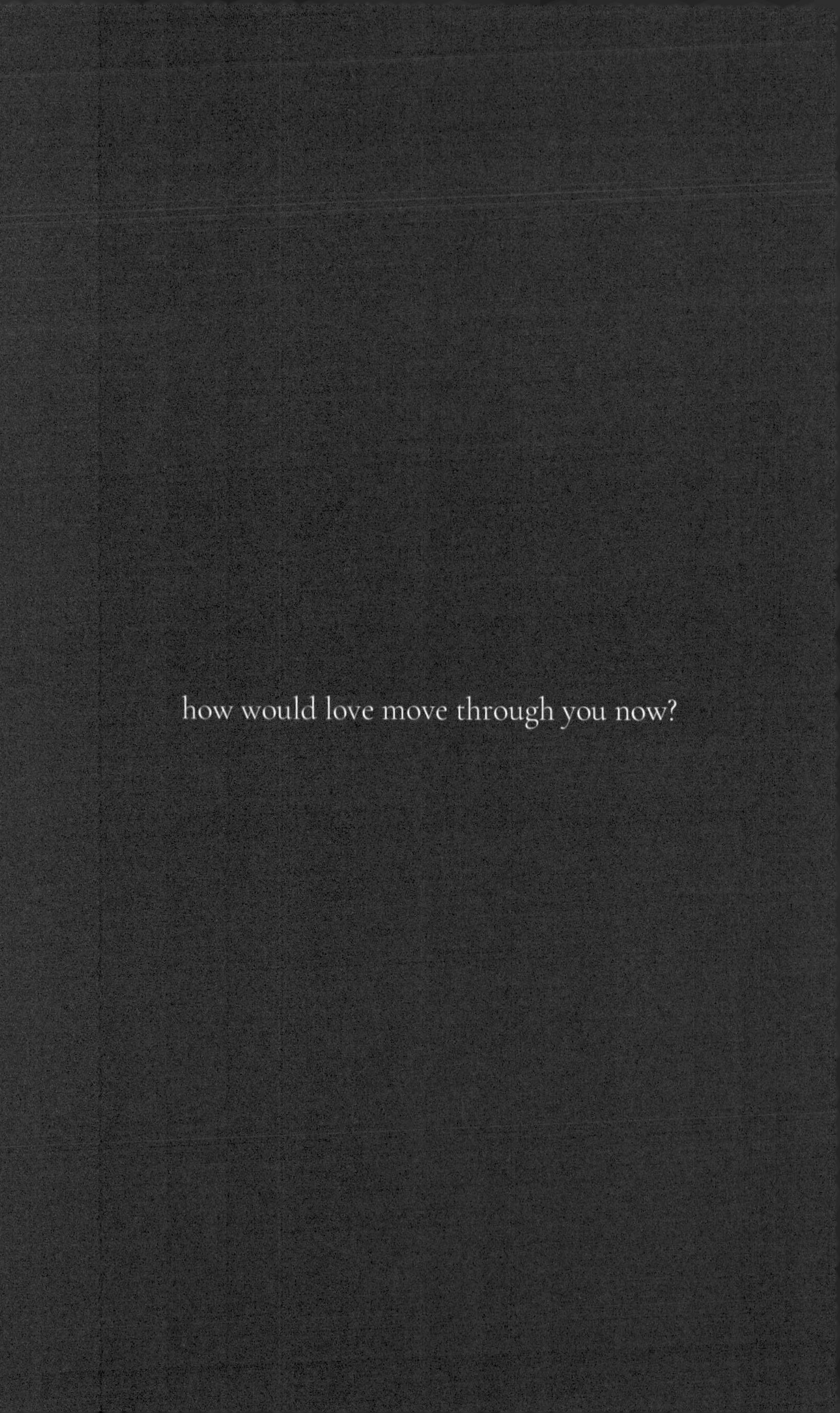
how would love move through you now?

where wounds can't reach

there is a place
somewhere deep
within you

a place
that has never
been hurt

somewhere
beneath
those raging flames
still starving
to find justice
for all those
bloody stabs
into this once so
innocent soul

somewhere
beneath
that unceasing pain
of what it means
to feel betrayed
and mistreated
by the ones
held closest
to your heart

somewhere
beneath
the tears
the blood
the shame
and
all those questions
of why and how
it could have ever
come this far

somewhere
beneath
the fear
trying to hold you
hostage
in a haunted house
of the shades
of what has passed

somewhere
there -
where even
the unforgivable
does not even need
forgiveness

because
what you truly are
can never
be hurt

because
your essence
can never
be harmed

because
love
can never
be broken

instead
we break
open
to the power
of love

and once
we return

return into
our center

and once again
open up
our heart

we are always
empowered

empowered
by love
itself

loving self

can you hold your self
the way you hold others
when they are breaking apart?

can you listen to your self
the way you listen to others
when it is raining in their minds?

can you speak to your self
the way you speak to others
when they forget their innermost
worth?

can you be there for your self
the way you are there for others
the moment they crave a hand to hold?

there is
so much love
in that little //
big lionheart
of yours

but can you dare
to love your Self
the way you love others
the way you love
this world?

mirrors

and when you open your eyes
everything you see
is a reflection
of the Self

and when you open your ears
everything you hear
is an echo
of the Self

and when you open your heart
everything you feel
is a mirror
of the Self

maybe that's the great paradox

that only
in the surrender
of yourself

everything
becomes
the
Self

and there -
from that space

seen through
the eye
of the soul

there's
no difference
any longer

between
loving yourself
and loving
the other

between
loving this world
and loving
the Self

love set in motion

and maybe
it's the fierce compassion
of the human heart
that will save us
in the end

maybe
it's a ripple chain
of random acts
of kindness
that will make
the difference
in the end

maybe
it's the courageous act
of daring to be present
with that seemingly
unbearable suffering
 - carried within
each and everyone of us -
that will liberate us
once again

maybe
it's the quiet rebellion
of coming together
- when all our difference
keep tearing us apart -
that will pave
the way
to peace
once again

maybe
it's the master weapon
of learning
to forgive
 - both ourselves
and one another -
that will heal
this earth
once again

because the truth is:
none of us
will make it through this
on their own

and the truth is:
every time
we chose
to bring love
into motion

 - through
our steps
our words
our breath -

we are choosing
the single
most powerful
medicine
to be served
through our
own flesh

into arms of love

but I have never left you,
my child

in your darkest hours
I was there

in your brightest moments
I was there

and I hear your cries
and you dreams
and your fears

and I see
how you are fighting
your way
through thicket
and thorns

devoted only
to follow
that call
of that fiery
warrior heart
of yours

but I promise you -
when you cannot
keep on going
any longer

I will be there
and I will catch you
when you fall

right
into
the
arms
of
love

sacred descent

and all of the sudden the darkness swallows you whole. she takes you. you and everything that you've ever thought you knew. everything that you've ever held onto. and she rips the ground on which you stood on just a second ago into a million tiny pieces. and as you fall – deeper and deeper into an unknown void – you watch your life falling apart. piece by piece. and everything you've ever thought to be true remains just as empty illusions quietly crumbling apart. you are lost. completely utterly alone. cut off from life, from love, from source. so far away from where you thought you belong. and even further away from where you wish you would be. you scream and you cry and you fight. you try to climb your way back out but the only thing that your trembling hands find is the bittersweet nothingness surrounding your entire being. the fear eats you. the pain breaks you. in ways you thought were impossible to even bear. to even feel. to even survive. the more you ask, the less you know. the more you fight, the more you lose. and every attempt to somehow fix this hopeless mess that your life just turned into – the more and more you break apart. all those demons you've tried to run away from all your life, come to gather around your naked, tired soul. and the snake comes to whispers to your torn open, bleeding feet. *welcome to the underworld. welcome to your sacred wound. welcome to your death.* but what she doesn't tell you yet, is that *this* is the greatest blessing you have ever received. that *this* is the great initiation into the wholeness of your being. that – yes – this may be your death, but it is also your rebirth into what you truly are.

beauty of the broken

somewhere
within the darkness
of your being
[that land of shadows
you're most scared
to journey to]

somewhere
within the valley
of your demons
[that underworld
where your deepest pain
is buried]

somewhere there -
the place
where your wholeness
is waiting

pieces
of light
 // hidden
fragments
of your
soul

waiting for you
to be re - membered
 - remembered
as the wholeness
of your being

come we
break
open
wide

there are treasures
hidden
in the darkness
of your body

like crystals birthed
from somewhere
deep within
the earth

breathe
into that space
and remember –

that all
of our roots
come from
the same place

[that dark womb
of all
of life]

come we
break
open
wide

there is grace
within the chaos
in the collapsing
of the known -
for the truth
of our essence
to arise

there is beauty
held within the depths
of our feelings -
within that courage
to experience
all those colors
of life

there's a blessing
within every wound
in the cracks
within our being -
allowing life
to touch our hearts
allowing love
to free us

as we
break
open
wide

allowing
all those
masks to fall -
for our vulnerable truth
to arise

come we meet
in the nakedness
of our tender
beating hearts

our greatest fear
and our deepest desire

a heart breaks open
and
love
flows
through

the holy breaking

let yourself
break open
by the suffering
of this world

let a roaring river
of tears
melt down
all those walls
that kept you
separated from
the whole

let it pierce
through
every bit
of numbness
that you've carried
in your cells

let the pain
be the guide back
into
the sacred
resurrection of
a soul
coming
back
to
life

until your body
becomes a temple
of both
earthly ache
and heavenly pleasure

until your
mere existence
becomes
a prayer
of embodied
liberation

something happens

something happens
when we stop
running away
from our pain
 - and instead
lovingly lean into it;
holding it
in the sweet embrace
of the presence
that we are

something happens
when we start
to breathe
into our pain;
when we follow
those silent cries
back to the roots
of our innate wounding

something happens
when we dare
to give voice
to our raw
tender
human
suffering

something happens
when we dare
to dance
the dance
with our sacred
shadow self
itself

when we dare to
hold the space
for that one
greatest alchemy
   of darkness
          into gold

something happens
 [sometimes quietly
sometimes roaring loud]
when we transmute
our inner worst enemy
into a sacred invitation
to o p e n
to f e e l
to b e
with *whatever* is
   alive

and from one moment
to another
that once
unbearable
human ache
becomes
 a s o f t
   s w e e t
    o p e n i n g
to none but
   life
   itself

breathable

it is okay

however you
are feeling
right now

it is okay

and not only that
it is
exactly
how you need to feel
right now

to learn
to embrace
whatever
there is

and suddenly
everything
becomes
bearable
breathable
breath returns
and we
remember

ALL IS PERVECT
JUST AS WE ARE

prayer of forgiveness

sacred waters
of forgiveness
wash us clean

may that balm
of fierce compassion
heal those wounds
hidden
in the shadow
of our collective
consciousness

may that wave
of purest love
carry the pain
back
back to its source

in the moment
we open our hearts
even to our darkest demons
even to our greatest fears

all those broken parts
of soul merge
back
back into light

all those fragments
of our being
coming
back
back into union

and in
that moment
of forgiveness
we are transformed

into our innocence
our original purity

that state of being
that has
never been touched
that has
never been hurt

and we
return home

where wounds
turn into power
and trauma
into love

by embracing
our deepest pain
we are choosing
our freedom

by facing
our deepest fears
we are freeing
our dreams

and only love remains.

who are you - when everything falls apart?

your refuge

let love be your refuge
when the storms
of changing winds
leave you
on a shattered field
of broken illusions

let love be your refuge
when those bonds
that kept you
in the comfort
of the known
are being cut down
by the sword
of truth itself

let love be your refuge
when the sharp
smoke of conflict
clouds your heart
and clouds your mind
trying to trick you
behind the veils
of separation

let love be your refuge
when there is nothing left
to hold onto
any longer
when once again
those hands
of trance
formation
stripped you naked
to your core

let love be your refuge
when the silence
of sweet darkness
is holding
your tired body
'cause this world
has turned
into a warfare
once
again

let love be your refuge

let her hold you
and support you
and nourish you
and heal you

and show you
that

even with
a broken heart
we can still
c h o o s e
t o   l o v e

and even
if we feel
all trust
abandoned us
we can still
 c h o o s e
   to trust
in those whispers
of the soul

and even
in the midst
of seeming
skin
breaking
division
we can still
 c h o o s e
   to meet
in what held us after all

lighthouse

visions held
in total emptiness;
lighthouses
of guidance
in that one
nocturnal sea

but if we are
a mere reflection
of galaxies
unfolding -
don't we
all carry
our own
northern star
inside?

the light we seek
to guide us home
is only found
within

a dialogue with death

and when death
comes knocking
at the door
of your consciousness

smile,
say:
welcome
and share
a cup of tea
or two

and when you
dare to look
deep into her
fiercely loving gaze
go on and ask
your one life-long
companion

what teaching
do you bring
to me
this time?

and watch her smirk
into her own reflection
in that drink
that you have served her

the one and only gift
that I ever came
to give:

to live this life fully
in unpostponable
radical
totality

for only the ones
that are willing
to meet death

will ever truly know
what it means
to be alive

to the warriors of light

this is for the warriors
fighting those hidden battles
in the darkest of the night

I see you.
I feel you.
I honor you.

and remember -
your secret superpower
lives right in the chamber
of the heart

and in the presence
of fierce love
even your demons
turn into allies

and even
in those moments
when the battle
tears you down

know that there's
a hidden gift
for all the
brave ones

that were left
by life
defeated

and were ready
to give up

and still
somehow
someway
made it
through

blessed by the battle

with a strength
that is u n b r e a k a b l e

a resilience
that is u n s h a k e a b l e

and a faith
that is u n t a m a b l e

and that deep
inner knowing that

*there is
grace
in it all*

that we can always
make it through

that even
in the darkest dark

*the light
always
returns*

these are
the blessings
of being
a warrior
of light

that
every battle
every heartbreak
every wound

is just
another invitation
to recognize

the light
it
lives
within

~

and when you're done
fighting your battles

and found the courage
to put down
your defenses
and surrender
your sword

then let us carry
that light
all together

to bring
those sparks of hope
onto the battlefields
of life

and hand in hand
we walk

as warriors
that learned
how to
love

from you to all

what if
your healing
was the healing
of this earth?

what if
each and every tear
you set free
is one with the raindrops
taming the fire
that burns
the forest
that keeps us
alive?

what if
those buried screams
that finally roar
from the depths
of your bones
is the liberation
of all those ones
whose voices
have never
been heard?

what if
by facing
your own shadows
you're bringing light
into the darkness
of our species'
collective
consciousness?

what if
breaking free
from your own trauma
means to free
your whole lineage
and all those ones
that will come
after you?

what if
by choosing
radical forgiveness
you are ending
a cycle of violence
you are choosing to be
- the turning point -
the beginning of
a new cycle
that one day
leads to
world
peace?

what if
learning to love
every little part
of yourself
is the beginning
of a revolution
birthed from
pure
unconditional
love?

what if
by claiming
the life of your heart's
sacred dream
you are birthing
the holy vision
that this earth
is longing
to be?

what if
by rewriting
your own story
you are
writing
a new story
for this entire
cosmos?

what if
this
is not only
an idea
not only
a mere poetic concept
of seeing the whole
within all?

what if
this
is exactly
how powerful
you are?

what if
this
is the only way
to change this world
from inside out?

what if
you
are the gateway
of the healing
of this planet?

rising into destiny

it happens quietly. when the sproutling breaks through the veil of dark and light. when the bud unfolds into the flower. when the butterfly's wings first open up to fly. when he tastes her nectar for the very first time. when the first day of summer return like the embrace of an old friend. when the sun rises. when the moon expands. when you arrive from your journey back home. even that moment before the early bird's song. it happens quietly. like the silence at the root of all creation. like that moment when you rise into your fully embodied expression. *but then – all of the sudden – all of creation is singing. all of creation is singing with you.*

sun returning

the sun is coming back,
she said

pouring through the cracks
of those walls
that we've built
around our souls

maybe
all those storms
and those earthquakes
all those wildfires
and tsunamis

they were not here
to destroy us

they were here
to free us

the sun is coming back

and only through us
breaking open

can the light
come back in

rising light

and when the sun
arises in the morning
she does not hide
her light

pouring all her colours
all over the horizon

all of her beauty
offered to this world

not scared
of being
too much
or
too little
or
of not being worthy
to take up
all that space

the ones
not ready to receive
the grace of her pure light
will simply stay asleep
in that moment
of unveiling

it's time to share your light
oh dear child
of the sun

or else
the night
it might continue

return to life

and there you rise

mud still sticking
on that naked
skin of yours

telling those stories
of all those
secret journeys
through your own
internal underworld

but if you learned
one thing
down there

then that
even dirt
is holy

and so
you paint yourself
both on that thorn kissed skin
and on your re-stitched soul

and there you rise
and there you go

and just for you
the serpent
sings
her sacred song

and just for you
dust and
rain and
fire
merge
to paint
a phoenix
into the sky

redefining selfishness

and if you ever
dare to doubt
those dreams
carved deep
into that skin
of your soul

or if those
breathtaking
desires
that keep knocking
on that door
of your heart

are not way
too selfish
to be formed
from your own
humble
hands

don't you see
that your vision
is nothing less
than holy?

and it's
your god given birthright

if not
your greatest responsibility

to free those dreams
from your own veins
and let them soar
across this world

'cause you were not created
to keep on playing small

and you did not come here
to die with
masterpieces
hidden
inside

'cause the expression
of your fullest potential
is the one single
greatest service
you'll ever offer
to the whole

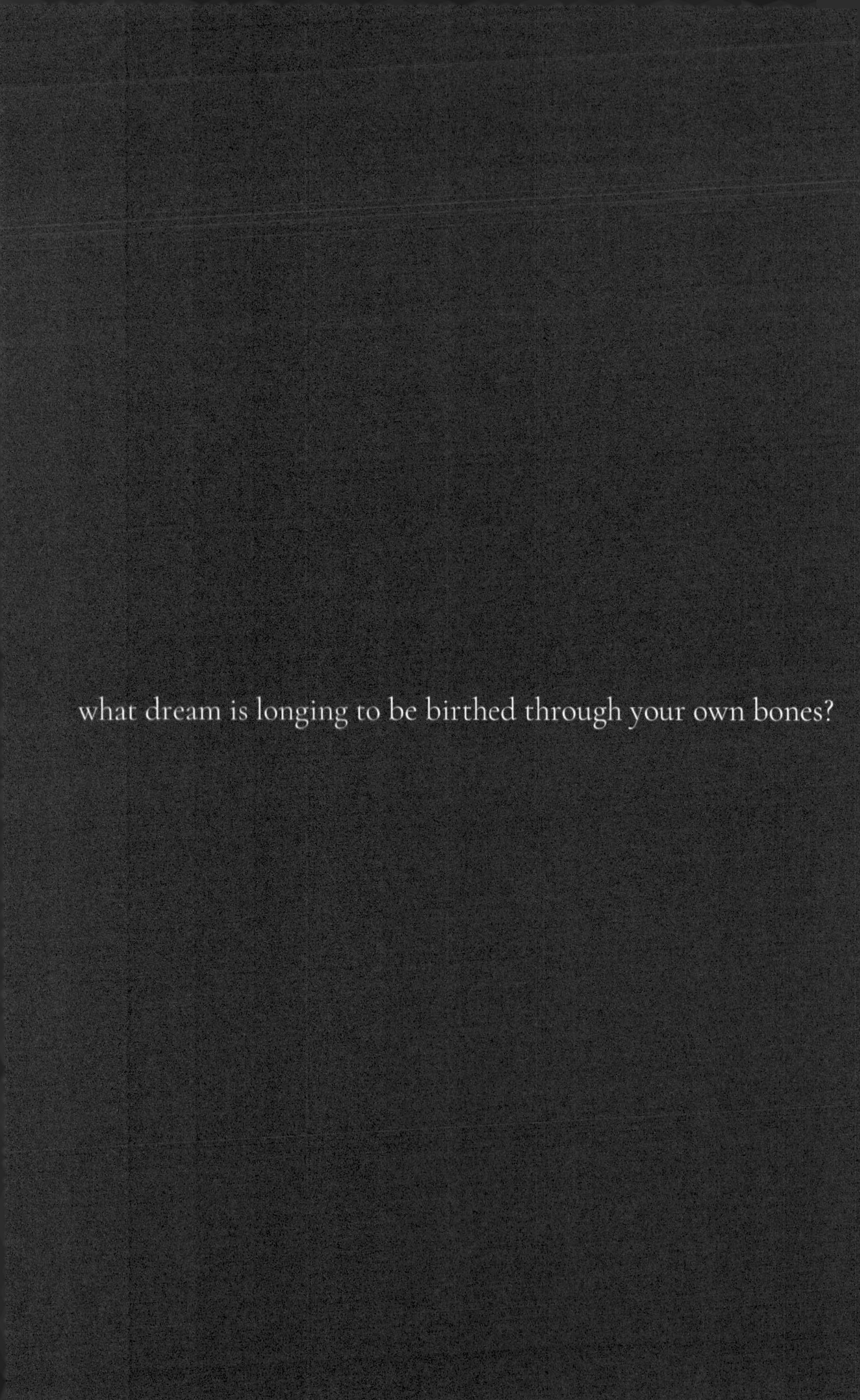
what dream is longing to be birthed through your own bones?

on the edge

some flowers
they blossom
in impossible
places

growing on the edge
of the cliff
of the waterfall

rooted only
in the cracks
of the stone

no choice
but to trust
in her place
in that circle
of life

this is
the power
of the creation
of mother nature

always playing
in that space

between the
ordinary
and the
unimaginable

and so
she teaches us
time and time
again

how our
unique beauty
is shown
by blossoming
right where we are
right as we are

even in the cracks
of our own
shattered
hearts

even in the gaps
between
the pieces
of torn souls

right in those spaces
that once
seemed to
trap us
in the hands
of fierce fate

yet isn't it
fate itself
pushing
our being

to rise into
our destiny?

expanding inside out

can you expand
beyond the limitations
of your own
little self?

can you see
past all those
stories of the past?

into a future
way too bright
for your own eyes
to realize

there is a world
waiting for you

build upon
infinite and infinite
of possibilities

a story
to be written
through you

as beautiful
and unknown
that not even
your wildest dreams
could describe

the impossible
whispers

I'm possible.

if you're willing
to let go
of any idea
how this life
should
be

you release
all your
resistance

and open up
to that greater vision
that longs
to be lived
through you

how scary
and how beautiful

that once
we fully open up
to life

all of life
lives through us
in us
as us

and everything
be – comes
     p o s s i b l e

choir of one

remember
that your voice
matters

the song
your soul
sings
is unique
to this world

there's only one
of you

even if
there's only One
at all

the great paradox
that isn't even one
after all

~

because if
one voice
is missing
in that choir
of the cosmos

how can we
ever hear
the fullness
of the voice
of the
One?

if only

if only you knew
how many souls
you have touched

just by being
what you're being

if only you knew
what you are giving
to this world

just by sharing
your pure presence

maybe then
you would see
how worthy you are

of living
all those dreams
you've silently been
dreaming
of

evolving into now

we could draw circles
in the sand beneath our feet
just as raindrops falling
expanding
uniting
dissolving
back in those waters
where all comes from
[as if nothing ever happened]

we could build castles
from splintered fragments
of those dreams
our hands once dared to carry
marvelous
shimmering and bold
castles without walls
for queendoms
beyond separation
where every heart pumps
royal blood
['cause isn't all of life
just sacred?]

we could live stories
that are far beyond
all limitations
of those glass cages
of imaginations
we did not dare to break
how beautiful
those shatters
of departed illusions
[reflecting piece by piece
those rays of rising suns]

because to thrive within
these times
of the great turning
costs the surrender
of the old
to the new

[THIS IS THE WAY
OF EVOLUTION]

every cycle comes around
like this planet
spinning round and round
herself

yet every moment
is so far
beyond
what could have ever
been possible

so why not
drop
all
of
those coulds
those woulds
those shoulds

and drop into
that limitless potential
cradled only
in t h i s
here & now

inner revolution

there is a revolution happening. silent as a mountain moving. unseen as a star being born. they do not show it in the television. they do not speak about it in politics. some may not even notice. until it arrives and shakes you up from somewhere deep within. *there is a revolution happening.* every time we breathe presence into the depths of our own hearts. every time we stop to listen to those soft whispers of the soul. every time we choose to open beyond the comfort of the known. every time we find forgiveness for all those scars that marked our path. every time we give up fighting against those demons of the self. every time we have the courage to stand up for the truth of our soul. every time we choose to love within a world that broke our hearts. *there is a revolution happening.* every time a woman reclaims the throne of her own sacred womb. every time a man dares to feel the pain carried in his bones. every time a human being drops the walls surrounding their heart. every time a soul decides to journey their own sacred way back home. every time an artist offers their labour of love to the world. every time a warrior remembers that the time of peace has come. every time a child is learning how to truly love oneself. every time a human realizes that their dreams are the prayers of god. *there is a revolution happening.* you cannot see it because it takes place hidden in the landscape of the soul. you cannot hear it unless you remember to listen to the rhythm of syncing hearts. but you can feel it. if you just dare to stop for a moment. close your eyes. take a breath. feel into your self. *there is a revolution happening.* and it begins right here – right here within the center your being.

call of gaia

the earth is calling you;
calling you
to rise up

into the truth
of your
courageous
open heart

into the wholeness
of all
that you are

through the shadow
into the light

the change is here
the change is now

right there
within you

and as the darkness
of this world
reveals itself

there is
no more reason
to keep hiding
your light

no more holding back,
my child

hear her whisper
from the core
of your bones

the world needs you
    y o u
and that medicine
you hold

in a time
that has been
poisoned
by fear

the only antidote
is love

dare to share

if one word
can shift a path

if one song
can save a life

if one soul
can change this earth

how can you
dare
not to share
your being
with this world?

re - dream

it is time
to dream
 n e w w a y s
into being

as old systems
are crumbling
between
our very fingertips

like falling leaves
and dead branches
being freed
by the grace
of the storm

making space
for the new
to become

can you smell
the taste of change
in the air?

of hungry flames
devouring all
that we thought
would keep us
safe

it is only that
which does not
serve us
any longer
only that
is ready
to fall

while the new
has yet
to be birthed
formed from
our own
naked hands

the only template
is that vision
hidden in the heart

who are we
in this world
if this world
is no longer
what we
have known?

it is time
to dream
 n e w w a y s
into being

to plant
those seeds
of love
right
in between
collapsing systems

it is time
for the
secret revolution
of those souls
still daring
to dream

because isn't the soil
the most fruitful
just after
the feast
of the wildfire's
flames?

it is time
for dreams
 t o b l o s s o m
from the ashes
of the old

resurrection

let's paint
masterpieces
from the blood
of wounded hearts

let's build
castles
from those fragments
of shattered dreams

let's weave
new ways
of being human
from all the lies
that we've been told

'cause there is nothing in this world
 [no matter how distorted it may seem]
that is no resource for the artwork of our being
that is no fuel for the revolution of the soul

peaceful warrior

can we stand
in our truth
while allowing
other points
of truth
to coexist?

and instead of seeing
the other
as wrong

can we listen
to one another
and understand
what life
looks like
from another
perspective?

instead of fighting
to be right
can we expand
in our own truth?

and from that bigger vision
 - seen through the eyes
of lived compassion

we can share
how beautiful
life is
witnessing
the truth
in every soul
we meet

*the secret weapon
of the
peaceful warrior
is to listen
from a
radically
open heart*

how can you be the change embodied
that you're awaiting for this world?

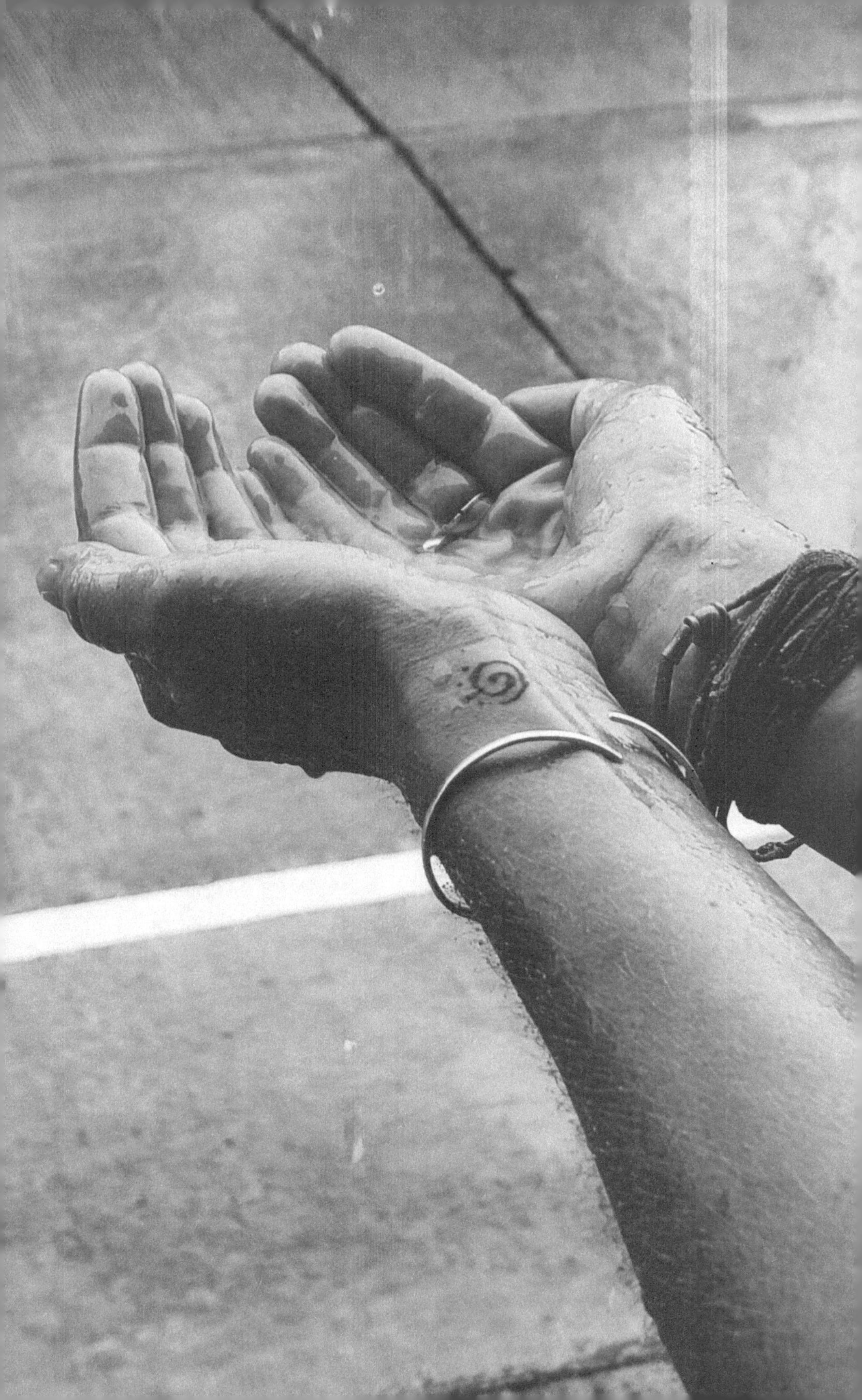

chosen ones

we are the ones
that came
to paint
new ways of
being human
onto the madness
of this world

a way
as ancient
as the primordial
heartbeat
of the earth

and as
the waves
of the
great change
leave the old
crumbling
apart

we burn
the times
of fear
and suppression
from our minds
and our own flesh

so that our being
and the being
of all beings
may once again
reclaim
our birthright
of true embodied freedom

we are the ones
to bring
the end
to separation

'cause in our love
even illusions
come to dissolve

*we are
the truth
that
reawakens
in the
remembrance
of the
soul*

the courage to jump

and one day
you realize

that you had it
within you
all along

all the courage
you need

to d o
the u n d o a b l e

to b e
the i m p o s s i b l e

to take
that breathtaking
leap of faith

that carries you

into
a
new
world

being revolution

t h i s   is
your permission slip

to break free
from those voices
echoing like broken records
from some distant past

telling you
you can't
you shouldn't
not you
not now

this is
the sign
you've been waiting for
all this time

the sign telling you
that it is time
  N O W

'cause in the end
is there any other moment
than this one
right now?

~

so, go on
and take that dream
cradled within
that tender cave
of your own chest;
silently fed
by those muscles
pumping life
through ever-
moving limbs

why else
would a dream
come to live
within this body
and this mind
if it wasn't
yours to live?

why else
should this heart
have kept beating
these lungs
have kept breathing
and those cells
have kept living
if there wasn't
a far greater
purpose
to it all?

why else
should this body
have carried you
through all of this

~ through all of those
hardships
and battles
and seemingly
never ending nights
of all seducing
darkness ~

if these hands
this belly
this voice
were not meant
to birth
something way, way bigger
than you will ever be?

why else
should you have survived
through all that you have
been through

~ even those moments
when you were right
at the brink
of giving up;
no longer seeing
any sense
to it all ~

why else
than
for you
to live?

and with that
I mean
live
   f u l l y

as if each and every moment
was the single
most precious gift given ~
your one and only chance
to meet life in radical totality

as if each and every breath
was your first breath and
your last breath ~
and yet another invitation
to let life kiss you from within

so let life kiss you
let life touch you
let life love you
   w i d e a w a k e

'cause why else
should there be
thousands
and thousands
of souls
standing
right behind you ~
the ones
that have birthed you
and all the ones
before you

and they have struggled
and battled
and starved
and suffered
and survived

just for
this one moment
in time

just in
the sheer hope
that one day
this one child
will wake up
and say

enough of this!

now
it's
time
to thrive

~

so, go on
and be that change
that irreversible
revolution

make that step
that leap
that move
that one single choice

to become
both
the embodiment
and the birthplace
of all of your
most wildest
dreams

because you can

and you deserve to

and because that's
e x a c t l y
what
you
are
meant
to
be

nothing in between

and there
you realize

that there
is n o t h i n g
in between
you
and
your dreams

 n o t h i n g
in between
you
and
love

 n o t h i n g
in between
you
and
the divine

the
only
separation -
the identification
of being separate
from life
itself

and there
you wake up
in the dream

and you
remember

*it has always
been
just
one
dreamer*

*no one less
than the creator
of this
dream*

belonging

maybe the true art of living lies in being so fiercely human and so utterly divine that the two return as one. to dance within that cosmic paradox of life until your very existence becomes a rebellion of truth, too vast for a mind to even grasp. to meet life with every breath as your one most cherished lover that could depart in every moment once again. to bow so many times at the altar of mortality that each moment starts to matter – even if nothing truly matters in the end. to run that wild and free upon this living body of earth until both soul and soil remember they've been one all along. to realize that we are all so uniquely special that being special is not even special anymore. to sink so deeply into the ordinariness of life that even divinity embodied in skin and in bones is nothing extraordinary any longer – because truly everything is. to find a piece of heaven within every little drop of rain that fell from grace [or fell as grace] just to make love to the earth. and to be just as that – a love story between the heavens and earth / the living language of belonging / the soundtrack of a journey of this one eternal home coming.

sacred reflection

hold a mirror
to your soul

what do you see?

can you see
your light?
your beauty?
your power?

can
you
see

your
 o w n
  d i v i n i t y ?

stardust

oh,
my dear
child of the stars,
you have come
a long way
to get here

infinite
of infinite
of cycles
around that
one cosmic sun

dancing soul
within the whirlwind
of creation ~
spiraling
to that rhythm
that beats
in everything
alive

all those ashes
and ashes
of stardust

painting
your skin
and flesh
and bones

all uniting
in this moment
for your being
to be formed

eternal stories
and stories unfolding ~
yet all there is
is just
right
now

that opens
limitless expansion ~
into a future
that is
right
here

can you feel it
in your being
that potential
that you hold

that divine force
of creation
forcing your being
to expand

bursting open
from your center
to pour out
into this world

*cosmos spirals
in your being
for new
starlight
to be
birthed*

pieces of light

just as the moon
reflects
the eye of the day
into black velvet realms
of night

it is the light
of the same sun
sparkling within
the eyes
of every soul
alive

one ray of light
carried within
every living being

just as
the stars
and the moon
and the sun

celestial bodies of light
born into the darkness
for one
to recognize
One Self

and as we look
upon this world
as that mirror
that it is

we recognize
our Self

in both the earth
and the stars

in both the moon
and the sun

in both the darkness
and the light

in both
the light
within our hearts

and
all those eyes
that witness
us

the returning

it is
a silent
homecoming

that moment
when you realize
that
home
has always been
within

there's no one
rejoicing
for the journey
that you've made

no one
  b u t y o u

there's no one
welcoming
you back
into their
warm loving embrace

no one
  b u t y o u

and yet
it's one
and the same
moment

that
you
welcome
the whole world
in your arms

because
once you remember

that
you
are
home
right here & now

you're recognizing
all at once

that
all of life
belongs
here,
too

already perfected

you are
a l r e a d y worthy

you are
a l r e a d y
unconditionally
loved

you are
a l r e a d y deserving
of everything that
your heart truly desires

you are
a l r e a d y
as whole
as anything
in this world
could be

stop searching
for yourself
  - as you
were never lost

stop trying
to fix yourself
 - as there is not
a single part of you
that is
in any shape or form
wrong
or broken
or shameful

it's only
that you
have learnt
otherwise

that you
were shown
otherwise

that you
were told
otherwise

that's it.

and so -
you have
forgotten

as simple
as it is

you've forgotten
your true nature

you've forgotten
what an
*intricately
perfectly
designed
piece of art*
you are

with
the same power
of creation
as that
primordial force
that once
created
you

innately worthy
innately pure
innately free

and nothing
and no one
in the whole
of existence
could ever
take that from you

as long
as you
remember

re - member
your own
Self

and
everything
that you ever
dreamed of

is already
with you

all the love
all the joy
all the peace

all the abundance
all the fulfillment
all the success

how else
could you
dream of it
otherwise?

it's already
right here
within you

a l r e a d y   h e r e
as what
you truly
are

all it takes
is to
re -
member

remember
t h a t
you
are

where do you belong - if not right here & now?

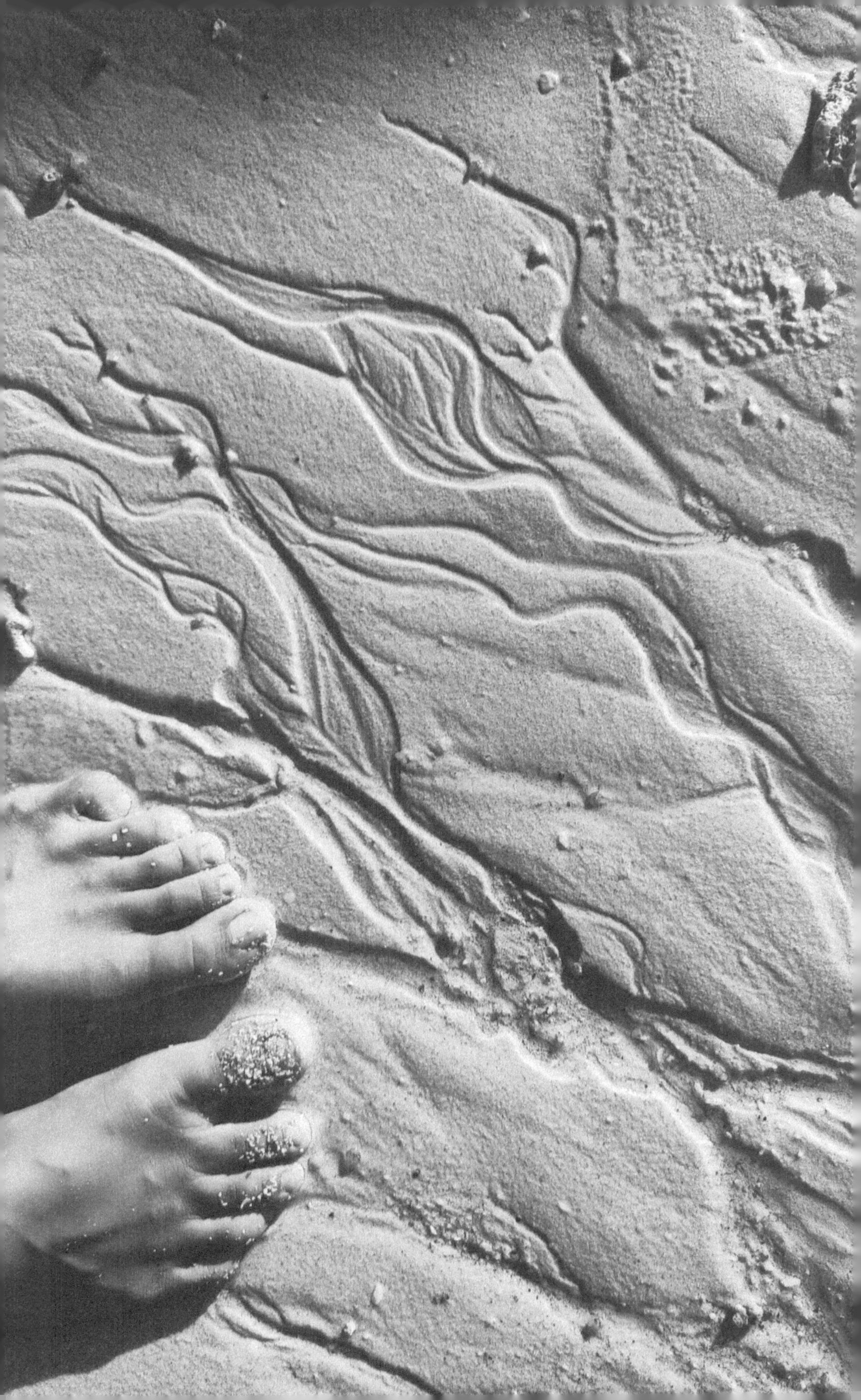

of trees and birds

and when
you see
a tree

can you see
yourself?

rooted
with your being
deep within
the earth

growing strong
and standing tall
as that breath of life
breathes you

~

and when
you see
a bird

soaring
in the sky

can you see
yourself?

riding
and rising
upon those changing
winds of consciousness

soul journeying
through space and time

and from
that higher vision

you are always free
you are always safe
you are never lost

because you know

that wings
were made
to fly

~

and when
you see
the bird
seeking shelter
in the branches
of the tree

can you see
your own self?

resting
in the sanctuary
of your being

cradled
in that home
that you are

soul
embodied
in flesh
and in bones

and as the bird
sings those hymns
of all those journeys
across lands and
across skies

even
the tree
remembers
what if feels like
to fly

on holy grounds

walk with reverence
on this ground
beneath your feet

each & every
particle
of dirt
on which you stand
is just as
alive
as

this skin
these veins
these bones
[that shape your life]

you are formed
from the very same
essence
as everything
you
touch

so, as you walk
this path
of yours

know your
feet are kissing
the womb of
your own mother

know that you
are walking
// and dancing
// and breathing
on living, holy grounds

song of becoming

becoming is
a strange song to play

with textures that taste
like nothing ever known
yet as familiar as
that time
you first heard
your own
soul
breathe

until one day you
might realize ~
each note
carries you back
where you
belong

cause even when
we've lost
our track

did we not know
all along

that
home
is not a place

it's the journey
of remembering

that
w h o
we truly are
is w h e r e
we truly come from

prayers to you

and I hope
you let the sound of the spheres
echo through that treasure box
of rib cage that you hold

and I hope
you let yourself dance free
upon your own winding road of soul ~
even if you still don't know
where all of this may lead to

and I hope
you keep uncovering your self
no matter if that gets
a bit messy at times;
believe me there are diamonds
hidden in the mud and dirt
and all of them
carry your name

and I hope
you don't let your spirit be tamed
by empty promises of a life
trapped in comfort;
cause even behind golden bars
one still lives in a prison

and I hope
you don't let your self be hardened
by those currents of
a seemingly cruel world
and even if it breaks you ~
keep breathing life into
your own tender heart

and no matter
what is present in there
~ what grief, what pain, what fear ~
never abandon
your own dreams,
'cause isn't that all
that has ever hurt you
after all?

and I hope
you stay devoted
to that extraordinary
essence of yours ~
and never ever compromise
the voice of your own soul,
'cause what else
have you got to lose
after all?

I hope
you stay
soft and wild and open and free
and please ~
never forget to remember
the love story
of creation
that you are

(no) journey home

you.
y o u .

I know you have come a long way to get here.
I know you have traveled across mountain ranges,
climbed peaks you thought you would never reach
and passed through valleys as deep and as dark
that they forever shaped your story.

and still, you are here.

I know you have crossed forests of confusion
and deserts of loneliness
and lost yourself in cities as big and as busy
that there wasn't even any space left to breathe.

and still, you are here.

I know you survived wildfires of pain
and thunderstorms of fear
and fought silent wars in the hidden chambers
of your own messy mind.

and still, you are here.

I know you have cried and laughed,
you have danced and ran and sing and played,
you have loved and defeated and fallen and risen
just like the everchanging tides of the sea.

and still, you are here.

and I know your hands are tired from always doing,
acting, achieving in this mad, mad theatre of life.
and I know your feet are tired of walking
and trying and t r y i n g and T R Y I N G
to reach in that one distant place, that they promised you -
where everything at last will be finally just fine.

but let me tell you one thing, my friend -
that promise was a lie.

you will never reach there.

because the truth is

you have already arrived.

and you can never reach there

because you have never left.

so, allow yourself to be here for just one moment
in that one eternal presence of that one eternal now
drop all of those masks for just one moment -
all those stories and names and faces
you've collected along your path

because beyond that -
beyond this busy, busy mind
and these oceans of emotions
beyond those wounds of what has passed
and all those worries of the future

there is a space - I'll meet you there.

a space as infinite as the vastness of the cosmos
a space as silent as the gaps between all words
a space as limitless, that everything is possible -
as it even birthed the possibility
of the creation of your life

it's the source of all that is
the no-thing-ness that birthed all of creation
and it's right here - in the center of your being

come home, my child, come home.

only that - there is nowhere to go to

'cause that space is the very essence of what you truly are.

breathe deep into that truth

y o u   a r e   a l r e a d y   h o m e .

Sarah Sameera (original birth name: Sarah Sanusi) is a poet,
singer – songwriter and practitioner of the healing arts.
She was born in Germany with Malay Singaporean roots but spent the
past few years living on the island of Koh Phangan, Thailand, where
the majority of this book was written.
Her creative work is deeply inspired by her intimate connection to
nature, the evolution of human consciousness and the mystical
experiences of her continual journey through the inner and outer
multiverses.

If you resonated with my poetry and want to support me in
spreading my message, feel free to recommend this book to
your loved ones and leave a review on amazon.
Thank you so much for receiving and supporting me!
It truly means the world to me ~
without you this dream of mine would not be possible.

Blessings & gratitude to your beautiful heart,

Sarah Sameera